GET INFORMED—STAY INFORMED

CARBON
TAX

Natalie Hyde

CRABTREE
PUBLISHING COMPANY
WWW.CRABTREEBOOKS.COM

Author: Natalie Hyde
Series research and development: Reagan Miller
Editor-in-chief: Lionel Bender
Editor: Ellen Rodger
Proofreaders: Laura Booth, Wendy Scavuzzo
Project coordinator: Melissa Boyce
Design and photo research: Ben White
Cover design: Katherine Berti
Production: Kim Richardson
Print coordinator: Katherine Berti
Consultant: Emily Drew, Public Librarian, B.F.A., M.S.-LIS.

Produced for Crabtree Publishing
Company by Bender Richardson White

Photographs and reproductions:
Front cover: Shutterstock; Interior: Alamy: 24-25 (Jim
West), 30 (Anthony Brown), 34-35 (Nature Picture
Library). Crabtree Publishing: cover image p. 10. Getty
images: 14-15 (Bradley Bermont/SCNG), 29 (Spencer
Platt). Shutterstock: heading band (testing), tablets
icon (Oleksiy Mark), key and graphics tablet images, 1
(jorik), 4-5 (Yermolov), 6-7 (Sundry Photography), 8-9
(Khairil Azhar Junoss), 10-11 (Syda Productions), 12
(wavebreakmedia), 13 (Jessica Girvan), 16-17 (motive56),
19 top (Sakoat Contributor), 19 bottom (Meinikof), 20-21
(Viktor Birkus), 21 top (Martyn Jandula), 22-23 (Thomas
Gilfeather), 26-27 (Aleksei Kazachok), 27 (Joe Clemson),
28-29 (Michal Urbanek), 30-31 (Sundry Photography),
32-33 (Monkey Business Images), 36-37 (Mark Agnor),
38 (Felix Mizioznikov), 39 (sittitap), 40-41 (Albachiaraa),
42-43 (metamorworks), 43 (Dean Drobot)

Diagrams: Stefan Chabluk, using the following as sources
of data:p. 7 ourworldindata.org/U.N. Global Carbon
Project. p. 15 U.S. Environment Protection Agency. p. 17
U.S. Carbon Tax. p. 18 legal-planet.org/NorthWest Energy
Efficiency Company. p. 22 Paris Agreement/International
Monetary Fund. p.26 The Conference Board of Canada. p.
30 Government of Canada/World Bank. p.35 The World
Bank. p. 37 Ecofiscal Commission, Canada

Library and Archives Canada Cataloguing in Publication

Title: Carbon tax / Natalie Hyde.
Names: Hyde, Natalie, 1963- author.
Series: Get informed--stay informed.
Description: Series statement: Get informed--stay informed |
    Includes bibliographical references and index.
Identifiers: Canadiana (print) 20210187689 |
    Canadiana (ebook) 20210187697 |
    ISBN 9781427150868 (hardcover) |
    ISBN 9781427150905 (softcover) |
    ISBN 9781427150943 (HTML) |
    ISBN 9781427150981 (EPUB)
Subjects: LCSH: Carbon taxes—Juvenile literature. |
    LCSH: Greenhouse gases—Environmental aspects—
    Juvenile literature. | LCSH: Climatic changes—Juvenile literature.
Classification: LCC HJ5316 .H93 2022 | DDC j363.738/747—dc23

Library of Congress Cataloging-in-Publication Data

Available at the Library of Congress

Crabtree Publishing Company

www.crabtreebooks.com   1-800-387-7650

Published in Canada
Crabtree Publishing
616 Welland Ave.
St. Catharines, ON
L2M 5V6

Published in the United States
Crabtree Publishing
347 Fifth Ave
Suite 1402-145
New York, NY 10016

Printed in the U.S.A./062021/CG20210401

CONTENTS

Climate change is a fact of life for all of us on this planet. Fighting climate change is a challenge because we have become so dependent on **fossil fuels,** the use of which is a main cause. We use fossil fuels, such as oil and gas, for everything from an ingredient in plastic to the energy to heat our homes.

" Carbon taxes . . . and similar arrangements to increase the price of carbon, are the single most powerful and **efficient** tool to reduce domestic fossil fuel CO_2 emissions. "

International Monetary Fund report, 2019

▶ Burning fossil fuels in industries such as this steel plant, or in furnaces and vehicles, creates **carbon dioxide** (CO_2) and other gases. As **emissions,** these enter Earth's **atmosphere** and are the main contributors to climate change.

QUESTIONS TO ASK

Within this book are three types of boxes with questions to help your critical thinking about our use of carbon tax. The icons will help you identify them.

THE CENTRAL ISSUES
Learning about the main points of information.

WHAT'S AT STAKE
Helping you determine how the issue will affect you.

ASK YOUR OWN QUESTIONS
Prompts to address gaps in your understanding.

SLOW TO CHANGE

Fossil fuels were formed from the remains of plants and animals that lived millions of years ago. The main fossil fuels are coal, oil, and natural gas. They are rich in the chemical element carbon. We burn fossil fuels to run our cars, send rockets into space, and create electricity. This creates **pollution**, which enters Earth's atmosphere. Switching to **renewable energy** sources, such as solar and wind power, sometimes stalls because the new technologies involved are often very costly to set up. **Consumers** stick with products they are used to because they are convenient, and people do not like change.

Governments are now increasingly looking for ways to shift our buying and using habits into those that are less harmful to the **environment.** Carbon tax is an attempt to shift the use of fossil fuels to renewable energy and **green technologies.**

IN THE KNOW

New plans, laws, and ideas have an impact on how we live and how our actions affect the planet. The more informed we all are about issues, the better our decisions will be. To do this, we need to gain skills in research, handling data, and knowledge backed up by scientific facts. Our understanding of climate change and the methods we adopt to slow, stop, or reverse it, such as carbon tax, depend on each of us getting good information and keeping up to date with new developments. It may also involve challenging companies and governments to introduce new measures.

Burning fossil fuels releases gases into the atmosphere that act like the glass windows of a greenhouse. They trap heat, leading to a **greenhouse effect.** One method some governments have used to lower **greenhouse gas** emissions is a carbon tax. This is an additional cost put on products that use fossil fuels. These include gasoline, jet fuel, heating oil, propane, and electricity created by coal-fired power stations. This issue, like many others, is **controversial**. Arguments center on whether a carbon tax will work or is fair. Collecting the most accurate and most **current** facts will help us decide what path to follow as we work to protect our environment.

Why do we need to stay informed? Data is always changing. As scientists and researchers gather **statistics** and results, we get a better idea of what methods might work to reduce our **carbon footprint** and the damage from climate change. Our understanding of the problem and its possible solutions is always under review. We can't rely on outdated facts. What we know affects our behavior. Knowing what laws to support, what politicians to elect, and what buying habits to change depends on the most current, accurate data.

MAKING THE BEST DECISIONS

When we don't stay informed, or if we don't have good information to rely on, we cannot make the best decisions. Speeding up climate change and the damage that results from it can have consequences on local communities, regions, countries, and continents. It is essential to look at how carbon tax may help control climate change. It is also important to examine arguments on whether it is effective and if there are alternatives to it. We must consider the pros and cons of each plan.

THE CENTRAL ISSUES

A tax on a product or service that is potentially damaging to society, communities, or individuals is called an excise or **vice tax.** For example, taxes on tobacco and alcohol are considered vice taxes. Why is the carbon tax considered by some to be a vice tax?

▶ Protesters gather at the September 2019 Global Climate Strike Rally in downtown San Francisco. "Tax the bads, not the goods" refers to applying the tax to activities and services, such as coal and natural gas power plants, that release the most carbon dioxide into the atmosphere.

CARBON DIOXIDE (CO2) EMISSIONS PER PERSON BASED ON USE OF FOSSIL FUELS

People living in the wealthiest countries of the world are, on average, the greatest consumers of fossil fuels. Many of these countries are the world's leading producers of fossil fuels.

| No data | 0 | 1 | 2.5 | 5 | 7.5 | 10 | 15 | 20 | >50 |

Source: https://ourworldindata.org/co2-emissions

Average figures in tons per year for 2018.

HOW TO GET INFORMED

It's sometimes difficult to know where to start your research when a topic is new to you. Understanding the different sides means getting to know the key players. In learning about carbon tax, the key players are fossil fuel/petroleum producers, governments, environmental groups, scientists, and consumers. Each key player has an opinion on whether a carbon tax is a good idea, will work, is fair to businesses and consumers, and will help slow or reverse climate change.

► Cycling instead of driving fossil fuel-burning vehicles eliminates greenhouse gas emissions. It also reduces **exhaust** fumes, noise pollution, traffic, and the need for more parking lots and roads.

It's not surprising that if you raise the price of something, people will buy less of it.

Christina A. Roberto, Ph.D., U.S. health policy expert, May 2019

THE KEY TO UNDERSTANDING

To fully understand carbon tax, it is important to review the changes in industry and in people's lifestyles that began the process of human-made climate change. Start by looking at timelines of how the Industrial Revolution increased the use of fossil fuels. Then examine how transportation across larger areas expanded from the 1900s on. Learning about the sequences of major events often helps to get a picture of how slowly or quickly the situation was created.

MAJOR SOURCES OF DATA

Key information about the use of fossil fuels can be found in many different places. Books, newspapers, and magazines, in print and online, can provide quick access to information. Industries that are affected by a carbon tax can provide details about their use of fossil fuels or steps they are taking to reduce carbon dioxide emissions. Government departments, such as the EPA (Environmental Protection Agency) in the United States or the Environment and Climate Change Canada department, form **policies,** create **legislation,** and provide statistics.

In reading reports and articles, it is important to understand the technical vocabulary and special terms that go with a topic. Carbon footprint, greenhouse gases, fossil fuels, and vice taxes (see page 6) are just some of the terms you will need to be familiar with to understand the carbon tax debate. Look at relevant glossaries, dictionaries, and key word lists to get clear definitions.

▶ Friends, classmates, teachers, and librarians can recommend Internet websites or articles they found on a topic. But, by doing your own research, you will make sure you get different opinions for a balanced view.

William Kamkwamba
Powering his Village

REMARKABLE LIVES REVEALED

Kylie Burns

◀ This book tells a true story of William Kamkwamba who, as a boy in Malawi, Africa, built a windmill to generate electricity to power his village. Reading about alternative energies can help us understand how the money from a carbon tax might help support such initiatives.

Sources of data can be written, oral, or visual. Written sources include reports and newspaper and magazine articles. Some written sources on the topic of carbon tax include promotional material from energy companies and new legislation by government environmental departments. Oral and visual sources might include TV documentaries and **podcasts** by environmental groups, or graphs and charts showing what carbon products will be taxed.

FACTS NOT OPINIONS

When looking at **source material**, you might notice that information may not be **impartial** but may have a slant toward one side of the debate. This slant of how and what information is selected or shown is called bias. Bias is not necessarily bad, but you need to recognize it so you can factor it in to how you read and understand the facts. For instance, reports from the fossil fuel industry may focus exclusively on the new technology it is using to reduce carbon emissions. Environmentalists may share a chart on the speed of melting ice in the Arctic. Business owners may focus on increased fuel taxes, and consumers will object to rising gas prices.

It is also important to find the most accurate and up-to-date information. To judge the quality of a primary source, historians use the Time and Place Rule. This rule states that the closer to the time and place of an event the material is created, the better the source may be. When you are looking for facts, not opinions, look for the five Ws of an article or report. A well-researched piece will tell you the Who, What, When, Where, Why, and sometimes How of the topic. Carbon tax is a relatively new topic, so there is a constant updating of data.

KEY INFORMATION

Primary sources are the original creators of information, for example a report on the amount of carbon dioxide released from a certain factory.

Secondary sources are reports, analyses, and interpretations of the primary sources, such as a magazine article comparing the carbon footprints of a range of industries.

Tertiary sources are **summaries** or databases of primary and secondary information. They include Wikipedia articles or entries in encyclopedias.

Source material on carbon tax is not hard to find. The Internet is a great place to start to gather information. Search engines can help you quickly and easily locate websites for organizations, charities, government departments, and industries affected by a carbon tax.

The Internet does have some pitfalls, however. You may have to pay to access scholarly websites. Some websites may look professional but are not **credible**. Popular theories that cannot be backed up with science might show up higher in search results than new studies or data. News outlets that are not **objective** may promote stories that only support their point of view. Others may issue false or fake news. The Internet can provide lots of good data as long as you are aware of these traps.

ASK YOUR OWN QUESTIONS

To determine if a source is credible, consider:
• Does the creator have solid credentials and expertise in the topic?
• Does the headline match the story?
• Is the publisher known to be reliable?
• What sources did the creator use?
• Is the source relevant and up to date?
• Is the source meant to be a joke or clickbait?

◄ At a library, many books and research papers can be examined in study rooms or remotely through the library's online portal as ebooks and databases.

▲ As our knowledge about the dangers of the use of fossil fuels increases, more people are questioning the way we live. In September 2020, protestors at this Extinction Rebellion rally in London, England, were demanding change.

GOING OFFLINE

Not everything is posted online. Printed materials, such as newspapers, magazines, journals, and textbooks, have a wealth of information. So, do the reports that the fossil fuel producers, energy companies, and large transportation industries have to produce each year for their shareholders and the government.

Television, blogs, social **media,** radio, and podcasts can give new viewpoints and personal stories of people who are struggling financially due to higher fuel prices, taxes, and emissions regulations. Organizations, businesses, and industry also often create advertisements and printed materials to show their side of the debate.

Governments create reports and statistics on climate change data and proposed changes before or after a carbon tax is applied. Scientific journals contain articles on how and where other countries have used carbon taxes and whether they have had any effect. These resources can be found in public and university libraries, archives, and government offices.

CONTEXT

When selecting and interpreting information, you should also consider the **context** in which source material was or is created. Context refers to the social, political, technological, and **economic** setting, or environment, of the time. An article written in the early 1900s about the massive growth in the fossil-fuel car industry would not have mentioned pollution, renewable energy, or climate change. However, every modern car magazine features low-emission and electric engines. Increasingly, we are hearing about carbon taxes in the news.

Taxes on carbon emissions are meant to help decrease, control, or eliminate climate change. But what is climate change? It is a change in long-term weather patterns. This happens when greenhouse gases trap warm air close to Earth, making worldwide temperatures rise. While our climate has been changing for hundreds of thousands of years, the causes were always natural events such as volcanic eruptions. The difference now is that most climate change is caused by human activity and is happening faster than ever before.

▶ Scientists agree that the increase in severe and frequent forest fires around the world, like this one near Los Angeles, California, on October 28, 2019, is almost certainly due to climate change.

Until there are penalties for emitting carbon, clean alternatives will just meet new energy demand.

Robinson Meyer, writer for *The Atlantic*, December 2019

GREENHOUSE GAS EMISSIONS IN THE UNITED STATES

Figures for 2018. Total emissions 7,360 million tons of CO_2

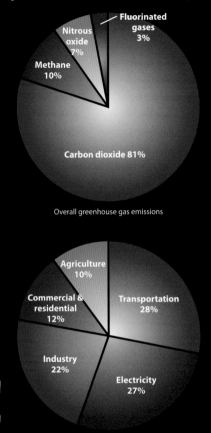

Fluorinated gases 3%

Nitrous oxide 7%

Methane 10%

Carbon dioxide 81%

Overall greenhouse gas emissions

Agriculture 10%

Commercial & residential 12%

Transportation 28%

Industry 22%

Electricity 27%

Greenhouse gas emissions by major sources of the economy

Percentages may not add up to 100 percent due to independent rounding.
Source: U.S. Environment Protection Agency

CARBON EMISSIONS

When we burn fossil fuels, carbon dioxide gas is created and released into the atmosphere. We use fossil fuels for heating, lighting, and cooling our homes, offices, and schools, and powering our vehicles and factories. As global temperatures rise, we can see the effects of climate change. Extreme storms damage coastal areas, threaten animal habitats, and cause seas levels to rise.

RUNNING OUT OF TIME

In most wealthy countries, people have begun changing their behaviors to limit and reduce climate change. They are turning to cleaner ways to generate electricity such as solar, water, or wind power. Electric cars are becoming more popular and less expensive. People are buying and using less plastic. Houses are being better insulated, and homeowners are switching to low-energy lightbulbs. But these efforts may not be enough. In less-wealthy countries, fossil fuels continue to be used, or are used increasingly, as they try to boost their economies and catch up with modern technology.

Climate change is still increasing and time is running out as more of our world and the life that depends on it are being destroyed. A tax on industries and activities that create carbon dioxide is one way governments are trying to bring about quicker and larger changes. It is based on the idea that using fossil fuels costs society in pollution, poor health, and environmental damage. A carbon tax will encourage people to move to new technologies and pay for these "hidden" costs.

A carbon tax works by including the environmental cost of using fossil fuels into the cost of goods and services that businesses and consumers have to pay. The price of gas at the pumps, electricity, and heating oil go up with a carbon tax. So do items, such as groceries, that are transported by trucks or trains that burn fossil fuels.

By switching to electric cars and greener energy, such as wind **turbines**, consumers pay less for the fuels they use. Hydro-powered electricity and local or farmers' market produce won't be affected by the tax. Governments and environmental groups believe that higher prices on fruit **imported** from other countries and vacations that include traveling by plane will encourage people to change what they buy and where they go. A carbon tax will alter people's lifestyles and habits.

▼ One criticism of the carbon tax is that not everyone pays their fair share. Airlines are often exempt from paying any tax, even though they are one of the biggest producers of carbon emissions.

ASK YOUR OWN QUESTIONS

• Should drivers of hybrid cars, which run partly on electricity from batteries, pay a carbon tax on the gas they use?
• Is it fair to tax drivers twice— for their car's CO_2 emissions and again with a carbon tax on their fossil fuel?
• Why might a carbon tax be higher for **diesel** fuel than for gasoline?
• If the electricity used by electric cars comes from burning fossil fuels, should the owners pay a carbon tax?

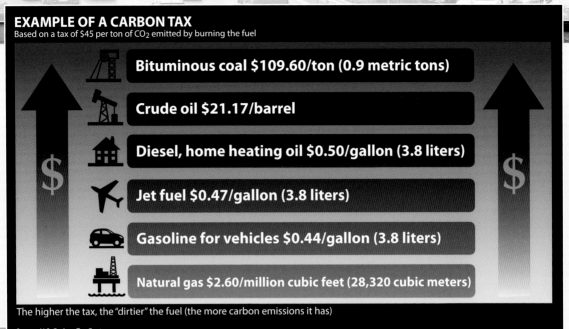

EXAMPLE OF A CARBON TAX
Based on a tax of $45 per ton of CO_2 emitted by burning the fuel

- Bituminous coal $109.60/ton (0.9 metric tons)
- Crude oil $21.17/barrel
- Diesel, home heating oil $0.50/gallon (3.8 liters)
- Jet fuel $0.47/gallon (3.8 liters)
- Gasoline for vehicles $0.44/gallon (3.8 liters)
- Natural gas $2.60/million cubic feet (28,320 cubic meters)

The higher the tax, the "dirtier" the fuel (the more carbon emissions it has)

Source: U.S. Carbon Tax Center

Starting next year, it will no longer be free to pollute anywhere in Canada.

Prime Minister Justin Trudeau, October 2018

RISING TAXES

A carbon tax would start low and increase over the next few years. At first, it would be a few extra cents at the pumps or on electricity bills. Over two or three years, that tax would almost double. Raising the carbon tax over several years would give consumers time to adjust to higher prices, or to find ways to move to renewable energy sources.

Researchers worry that the consumers hit hardest by higher prices will be low-income households. People already struggling to pay bills may have real difficulty paying even more for groceries and fuel. To help individuals handle the increased cost, governments often issue a **tax rebate**. This refunded amount is supposed to offset the extra costs they will pay throughout the year. Even though at the end of the year most people should have all the money refunded, governments hope that having to pay upfront will still encourage them to move to cleaner energy and local products.

While a carbon tax is widely used around the world to encourage a shift to green technology and a change in how much we use fossil fuels, it isn't the only **incentive** governments use. Cap and trade is a system in which governments set limits on emissions for industry. Each year, that limit can be lowered to continually decrease carbon emissions. The total amount of emissions is divided into fixed shares called quotas. There is a set number of quotas. The government gives each industry a quota, or limit. It keeps some emissions allowances aside and auctions them off to industries that want more. Those industries can sell unused quotas to other industries. The cap-and-trade system is used within each state and province, by whole countries, and on a global market.

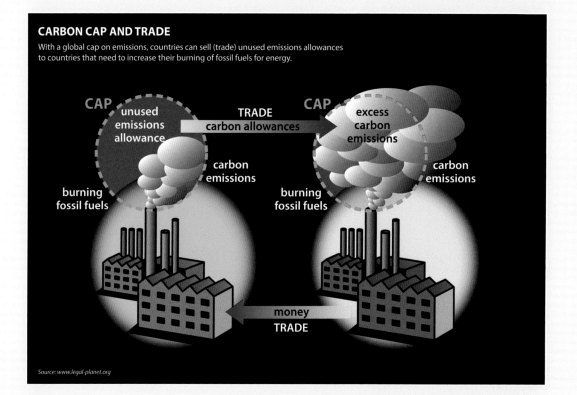

CARBON CAP AND TRADE

With a global cap on emissions, countries can sell (trade) unused emissions allowances to countries that need to increase their burning of fossil fuels for energy.

CAP — unused emissions allowance — TRADE carbon allowances — CAP — excess carbon emissions — carbon emissions — burning fossil fuels — carbon emissions — burning fossil fuels — money TRADE

Source: www.legal-planet.org

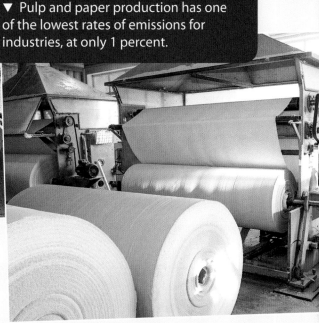

◀ Cement is the source of about 8 percent of the world's carbon dioxide emissions. Cement is the main ingredient in concrete, which is the most commonly used human-made material on Earth.

▼ Pulp and paper production has one of the lowest rates of emissions for industries, at only 1 percent.

Cap and trade can be an effective way to make sure the amount of carbon emissions decreases to meet pollution-reduction goals. To control their costs, industries are **motivated** to find ways to use less of their quotas. These can include investing in new technologies or finding more efficient ways of manufacturing.

TRIED AND TESTED

Cap and trade is not a new idea. Since the 1980s, it has been used in the United States to restrict dangerous gases, such as sulfur dioxide (SO_2), that create acid rain. Acid rain kills vegetation and aquatic life, damages stone buildings, and makes soil less fertile. Cap and trade has almost halved acid-rain-forming emissions in the United States. Tokyo, in Japan, also uses cap and trade to control and reduce energy use and carbon emissions. Since it started the program in 2010, it has lowered emissions by 25 percent from emissions levels in 2000.

Both carbon tax and cap and trade have pros and cons. Cap and trade allows each government to set definite goals in lowering carbon emissions. But it takes time to set up and get working. A carbon tax is an easier system to put in place and becomes effective quickly.

For residents, a concern about carbon tax is what the government will do with the money it raises. Each area makes its own rules about how that tax money is distributed. Most countries set aside some or all of the income to improve the public's health and education, or for clean energy research.

Currently, the United States does not have a federal carbon tax. Some cities or counties in different states have put their own carbon tax in place. These include Boulder, Colorado; Montgomery County, Maryland; and the San Francisco Bay Area in California. Eleven states, including California, Maine, New Jersey, and other northeastern states, have created the Regional Greenhouse Gas Initiative (RGGI). This program uses cap and trade rules to limit carbon emissions. The state of Washington has its own Clean Air Rule to cap emissions.

All provinces in Canada have a carbon tax. For most people, they will receive that money back as a rebate. The rest of the collected tax will go to small businesses and organizations to help them cover the increase in their costs.

THE CENTRAL ISSUES

When switching to new renewable energy products isn't possible, the carbon tax also encourages consumers to lower their energy use. Why is promoting energy efficiency important?

▼ Oil refineries, like this one in Alberta, Canada, are finding that having a solid plan to reduce carbon emissions doesn't just help lower carbon taxes. Initiatives that reduce damage to the environment also attract investors who provide money to improve energy production.

▲ Luxembourg in Europe has become the first country in the world to offer free public transportation. The government hopes free train, bus, and tram rides will reduce pollution, traffic jams, and fossil-fuel use.

ENCOURAGING CHANGE

So how can a carbon tax work if most of the money is returned to users? Supporters of the tax say bigger industries that don't receive rebates will be the first to seek out new ways of manufacturing and running their businesses to reduce costs. Consumers may get back all the extra money they've spent at the end of the tax year, but it may still encourage them to make changes as they face higher prices for gas, energy, and groceries. For example, not buying expensive cauliflower trucked in from far away, but buying locally grown carrots instead, will reduce emissions.

A portion of carbon tax dollars may be spent on projects to create new technologies that reduce our need for fossil fuels. Some programs help schools replace old windows or install solar panels. Critics say for a carbon tax to have a really big effect on reducing climate change, the price has to be much higher and that will have a negative effect on the economy.

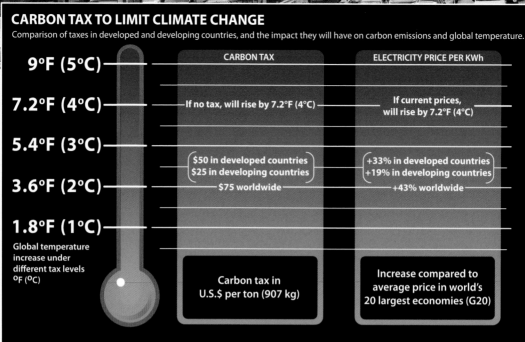

CARBON TAX TO LIMIT CLIMATE CHANGE

Comparison of taxes in developed and developing countries, and the impact they will have on carbon emissions and global temperature.

Global temperature increase under different tax levels °F (°C)	CARBON TAX	ELECTRICITY PRICE PER KWh
9°F (5°C)		
7.2°F (4°C)	If no tax, will rise by 7.2°F (4°C)	If current prices, will rise by 7.2°F (4°C)
5.4°F (3°C)		
3.6°F (2°C)	$50 in developed countries / $25 in developing countries / $75 worldwide	+33% in developed countries / +19% in developing countries / +43% worldwide
1.8°F (1°C)		

Carbon tax in U.S.$ per ton (907 kg)

Increase compared to average price in world's 20 largest economies (G20)

From Paris Agreement 2016 and International Monetary Fund

▼ Scotland generated 90 percent of its electricity with renewable energy in 2019. It is on track to meet its goal of 100 percent electricity generation from wind, solar, and tidal power in the next year or two.

▲ In Sweden, you can rent an electric car like this one at a solar-powered charging station. This can help people who cannot afford to buy an electric car to still be able to use green transportation.

Governments in some areas think a carbon tax alone is not enough to curb greenhouse gases and slow climate change. They are concerned that industries are paying all the tax and consumers are not shouldering enough responsibility. Others think that a carbon tax needs to be combined with other incentives to really be effective.

GREEN NEW DEAL

The United States is divided on how effective a national carbon tax would be. A proposal called the Green New Deal has been put forward by Congresswoman Alexandria Ocasio-Cortez of New York and Senator Edward Markey of Massachusetts. Its goal is to move the United States away from relying on fossil fuels and carbon emissions. The plan aims to source 100 percent of the country's electricity from renewable power in the next 10 years.

The Green New Deal also calls on the country to upgrade every building to be more energy efficient and to use electric vehicles and high-speed rail systems. It would also provide training to help people find work in new **green energy** technology if they lose their jobs in fossil fuel industries. Some argue the deal will be too expensive, but have not come up with their own plan to replace it.

ALTERNATIVE PLANS

Some countries, such as France, Denmark, and the United Kingdom, have plans to ban or **phase out** the sale of new gas and diesel cars and vans by the year 2050. Several critics of carbon taxes say a similar phase out on coal-fired plants, gas stoves, and oil drilling is necessary. Other countries and some American states also have rules that a certain percentage of power must come from renewable energy. By raising those amounts, areas would be forced to move completely to renewable energy by a certain date.

KEY PLAYERS

The **Intergovernmental Panel on Climate Change (IPCC)** is part of the World Meteorological Organization in partnership with the United Nations Environmental Programme. This panel recommends much higher carbon taxes than most countries have planned—as high as $200 per ton of CO_2 emissions by 2030. Critics worry this could lead to soaring gas prices.

23

When you start to form an opinion about a topic, it is easy to look only for source material or other opinions that agree with your point of view. To really understand a subject, it is important to consider other perspectives. Ask yourself why there is controversy concerning the topic. Is there any **merit** to the problems or flaws that other sides of the story reveal?

WHAT'S AT STAKE?

How important is it that we lower our carbon emissions quickly? What might happen if we wait for a solution to carbon emissions that is better than a tax on products and services?

LOW RISK   HIGH RISK

Finding solutions to greenhouse gas emissions, such as carbon dioxide, and their effect on climate change is not straightforward. Many parts of society, including transportation, health, **natural resources**, and electronics, are affected by our use of fossil fuels. The reason governments want to move slowly with big changes is because they will negatively affect the system of jobs, industries, and businesses that keeps money flowing. That will make them unpopular with citizens, who generally do not like being forced to change their ways.

IMPACT ON THE ECONOMY

A carbon tax affects the economy by reducing money in consumers' pockets. It may also reduce demand for products, such as refrigerators and TVs, that are currently created with a high carbon footprint. This in turn might increase the number of unemployed people. Some researchers argue that these problems would not last long and that greener product models and new green industries would take their place and create new jobs. They point to Sweden as an example. Sweden has the highest carbon tax in the world, but the economy there is strong. Studies show that most people agree that governments should reduce greenhouse gas emissions even if other countries do not.

Around the world, young people in particular are becoming more active about climate change, environmental damage, and how we must take steps to reduce our dependency on fossil fuels. Widespread use of carbon tax can be a great tool.

◀ Switching to new industries that are not dependent on fossil fuels will also mean restructuring the economy. Countries that do not plan for this or create new opportunities for workers in green industries will experience more job losses and more workers using charity and food banks, such as this one, to feed their families.

One of the biggest worries with taxing carbon emission-producing industries and products is how it will affect businesses. For businesses such as car manufacturing, the effect could mean a factory might be moved to an area with a lower or with no carbon tax. With fewer sales to consumers, it could also mean cutting jobs or wages at the factory.

A GLOBAL MARKET

With imported goods, such as furniture and plastic items, a carbon tax will make them more expensive. Consumers will look for cheaper alternatives, leading to lower sales for importing companies. This could result in businesses closing and going bankrupt.

With online shopping becoming more popular, consumers may find it cheaper to buy from an international company in a country that does not have to add a carbon tax to have goods shipped. This will have an impact on local companies that keep people in their communities employed.

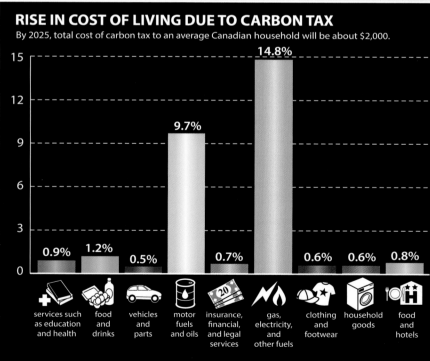

RISE IN COST OF LIVING DUE TO CARBON TAX

By 2025, total cost of carbon tax to an average Canadian household will be about $2,000.

services such as education and health	food and drinks	vehicles and parts	motor fuels and oils	insurance, financial, and legal services	gas, electricity, and other fuels	clothing and footwear	household goods	food and hotels
0.9%	1.2%	0.5%	9.7%	0.7%	14.8%	0.6%	0.6%	0.8%

Source: The Conference Board of Canada

◄ Auto industry experts say the increase in gas prices due to a carbon tax shouldn't affect consumers much because cars have increased in fuel efficiency over the past few years. But they are worried that higher-priced cars will mean fewer new cars sold. This may result in layoffs for workers.

FROM OLD TO NEW

Many researchers take a more positive view of the impact a carbon tax will have on the economy. They say that new, greener industries and cheaper local produce will mean new stores, farms, and industries will be created. This will lead to new jobs. Employees in a coal-fired power plant could be retrained and certified to work in solar- or wind-**power-generation** plants. Automotive industry workers can shift into electric car manufacturing. The key is the need for governments to support retraining, encourage banks to finance new businesses, and to set up networks of electricity charging points for vehicles across all countries.

A few experts claim that the effects of yet more climate change will have a far worse impact on the economy than a shift to new technologies and industries. Increasingly severe storms, droughts, flooding, winds, and rising seas levels are affecting crops and animal feed, which can lead to food supply shortages.

▶ Polls in the United States show 87 percent of small business owners are against a carbon tax. They say they will be contributing almost 50 percent of the taxes collected but will receive only about 7 percent back in grants and rebates. Only a fraction of these new costs can be passed on to customers, so the business will lose profits.

27

Environmental groups and organizations work to slow or end human-made climate change. Their focus is to encourage governments to change laws and consumers to change their spending habits and behaviors. While these groups believe any way that limits carbon dioxide or any other greenhouse gases is good, not all of them support a carbon tax. In their eyes, the changes that come from taxing carbon emissions happen too slowly. Climate change is an **urgent** problem, and they argue we cannot afford to wait while industries and the public shift away from carbon-dependent products and services.

WHAT'S AT STAKE?

How do climate change protests and marches affect the message of the problem's urgency? Is it more or less effective than other ways of communicating such as social media, podcasts, articles, or news coverage?

▼ Young people in Vancouver, Canada, raise awareness of the impact of climate change.

28

◀ At the United Nations Climate Action Summit in 2019 young activist Greta Thunberg told leaders that they are not doing enough to stop and reverse climate change. She told them she does not think that countries are cutting carbon emissions fast enough.

Another problem environmentalists see with using a carbon tax to slow emissions is how the public may respond. They worry people will see the tax as a simple solution. It may be easier to just pay more for items than to make difficult changes in how they travel, and what they eat and buy. Most environmentalists believe a carbon tax needs to be combined with other incentives. These include firm dates for companies to switch from making gas cars to electric cars, or closing coal-fired power plants to move to solar and wind farms.

FOCUS ON NATURE

Another sector with strong environmental focus is **Indigenous** groups. Because of their culture of living close to the land and relying on natural resources, plants, and animals, they are some of the people who are hardest hit by climate change. Indigenous peoples believe that all people and governments should be stewards of the land and protect the planet from climate change. Indigenous groups in Canada are pressuring their government to honor its commitment to international goals of reducing greenhouse gas emissions. Some tribal leaders in the United States are working on their own carbon tax legislation because they feel they are running out of time to stop a climate change disaster.

Consumers often see prices going up. Fuel costs, insurance premium increases, and natural disasters already affect the price of our food and supplies. The question some researchers ask is, will higher prices due to a carbon tax actually change people's buying habits?

TAX AND REBATES

The biggest increases for the public will be the prices of gasoline and electricity. Those who can afford electric cars or to put solar panels on their homes will likely be motivated to make that change. Governments offer incentives to encourage homeowners and landlords to fix leaks, improve insulation, and install smart gas and electricity supply meters.

What about people who are already struggling to live on their incomes? Many can't afford the high price of renovating, installing a new power system, or buying a brand new car.

▲ Smart meters allow homeowners to monitor their fuel usage and carbon emissions and send readings wirelessly to power stations, reducing site visits from recorders.

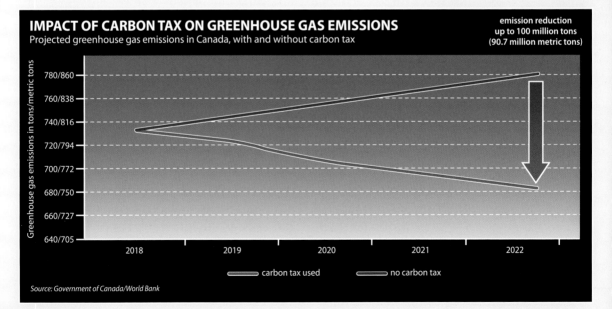

IMPACT OF CARBON TAX ON GREENHOUSE GAS EMISSIONS
Projected greenhouse gas emissions in Canada, with and without carbon tax

emission reduction up to 100 million tons (90.7 million metric tons)

Greenhouse gas emissions in tons/metric tons

780/860	
760/838	
740/816	
720/794	
700/772	
680/750	
660/727	
640/705	

2018   2019   2020   2021   2022

⬭ carbon tax used   ⬭ no carbon tax

Source: Government of Canada/World Bank

▲ This new housing development in San Francisco, California, is covered in solar panels. About 6 percent of U.S. residents had installed solar panels by 2019, but another 46 percent are considering installing them in the future.

They will be the ones negatively affected by a carbon tax. The Canadian Government argues that this is why they are offering a tax rebate. Lower-income earners worry that the tax rebate may eventually end over time or end with the election of a new party to the government.

BUDGET BUSTING

With a carbon tax, food and other products that are imported using fossil fuel-burning vehicles will also have higher prices. Examples include bananas shipped by trucks, frozen seafood carried by planes, or rice transported by trains. Fruits and vegetables that are out of season and grown in warmer climates will have higher prices. This will make it harder for low-income families to afford a healthy diet.

Furniture crafted overseas is often cheaper to make because wages in other countries are much lower than in North America. A table made locally is great for the environment and for local jobs, but likely costs more to make. The higher prices may push even more families below the **poverty line** if they can't afford necessary items. This could lead to money raised from carbon taxes being spent on welfare services and not on combating climate change.

5 WHERE THINGS STAND

Topics, such as whether to use a carbon tax to fight climate change, are constantly changing. Scientific studies, expert opinions, new laws, and a changing environment all give us new information. To get informed and stay informed, you must track these changes and refresh your knowledge regularly.

▶ A carbon tax will affect the prices of items you may not think of as having a large carbon footprint. Fabric and even finished clothing are often imported from overseas. The fuel needed to transport these items contributes to climate change.

What are the economic and environmental benefits of having most or all countries adopt a carbon tax?

> It's not a question of carbon pricing [tax] or nothing. It's a question of carbon pricing or regulations, carbon pricing or subsidies, and from an economist perspective, it's pretty clear that carbon pricing is the lowest cost way.
>
> Dale Beugin, Executive Director of Canada's Ecofiscal Commission, 2018

SPREADING MISINFORMATION

Sometimes studies haven't been done carefully, experts don't have the best **evidence** or experience, or source material is heavily biased. If someone shares this data, they can spread misinformation. Occasionally, people who believe one side in a debate are so eager to be correct that they look only for information that supports their view. They may not check their sources carefully. In some instances, they might even spread misinformation on purpose. It is **vital** to be aware of this and, before you share any data, always double check that it is as up to date as possible.

The issue of carbon emissions and how to reduce them is a worldwide problem. If one country or area is not working toward ending this, the overall success is in doubt. So far, there is a national carbon tax in 25 countries. Forty other countries have some sort of price on carbon, either with a cap-and-trade program or by taxing certain industries. Finding out how well carbon taxes are working around the world can help plans to handle the problem in your own area.

THE PARIS AGREEMENT

The Paris Agreement is a UN initiative to fight climate change. It was signed in Paris in 2016. Most UN members signed it, including Canada and the United States. The U.S. left the accord in November 2020, and rejoined it in January 2021, after electing a new government. Its goal is to reduce emissions to keep the average global temperature from rising. Under the agreement, each country creates a plan to reduce the rate of their greenhouse gases.

The biggest argument against a carbon tax is that it may work for a while, but it is a **short-term** fix. To really solve the problem of greenhouse gas emissions and climate change, we need to switch from fossil fuels to renewable energy. But how do we do that without throwing millions of people into unemployment and poverty? Researchers say the switch will take four steps.

- *First, develop new technologies.* Hydro-electric power works well but is limited to areas of high rainfall or reliable high tides. Solar and wind power generation still have some problems. This renewable energy can be created only when the sun is shining and the wind is blowing. There has to be a large and reliable storage system to save energy for use when it is dark or windless. Scientists are still working on improving how much energy batteries can store and for how long. (Nuclear power is an option in some countries but its costs are great and there are environmental concerns.)

- *Second, new technology has to be affordable.* Right now, most people cannot afford to install solar panels or solar shingles on their roofs, or to buy electric vehicles.

- *Third, structures to support renewable energy must be built.* These include charging stations for electric cars, an updated power grid, and new designs for houses, offices, and schools.

- *Fourth, there needs to be new technology to offer better service and a lower cost than the older technology.* If solar shingles or solar panels cost the same or less than normal asphalt shingles, and electric cars were a lot cheaper, people would switch.

▶ BedZED (Beddington Zero Energy Development) is a housing development in London, England. People can live and work there comfortably without contributing to carbon emissions. It is a carbon-neutral complex. It produces as much energy from renewable sources as it uses. BedZED includes 197 residential homes, 14 apartments, as well as workspaces, stores, a café, sports facilities, childcare, and a health care center.

Critics say that a carbon tax does not help society move through these four steps except for some temporary help with the second step. They say any money from a carbon tax should go toward development of new renewable energy technologies and **infrastructure**.

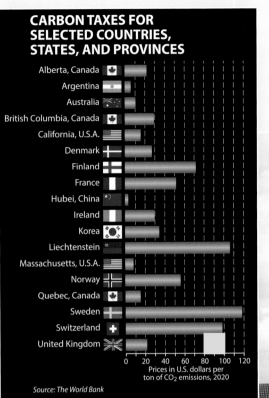

CARBON TAXES FOR SELECTED COUNTRIES, STATES, AND PROVINCES

Alberta, Canada
Argentina
Australia
British Columbia, Canada
California, U.S.A.
Denmark
Finland
France
Hubei, China
Ireland
Korea
Liechtenstein
Massachusetts, U.S.A.
Norway
Quebec, Canada
Sweden
Switzerland
United Kingdom

0 20 40 60 80 100 120

Prices in U.S. dollars per ton of CO_2 emissions, 2020

Source: The World Bank

Myths are pieces of information that are repeated so often that people assume they are true without checking. It is a good idea to double check common beliefs to make sure they are based on facts that can be proven.

The debate concerning a carbon tax has also produced some myths:

Only a really high carbon tax will have an effect.
Years of data show that any level of carbon tax does change people's buying habits. Carbon taxes have been put in place in more than 25 countries and the evidence given by researchers is that even low to **moderate** carbon taxes have reduced carbon emissions.

A carbon tax will hurt jobs.
It is true that jobs in heavy carbon-dioxide-producing industries may begin to disappear as demand for fossil fuel-based items and services fall. But demand for products and services from renewable energy will increase and cause more jobs to be created. With retraining, people who have lost their jobs should be able to find new jobs.

Carbon tax hurts businesses, but big polluters are exempt.
Many governments cycle money collected from carbon taxes into programs to help small businesses adjust to new prices. Large carbon dioxide emitters are not exempt and are taxed on how much they emit. This is done to keep them competitive in a world marketplace and not produce any sudden shifts in the industry that will cause problems with the economy.

ASK YOUR OWN QUESTIONS

What are some things you have heard about climate change or carbon taxes. How can you determine if they are factually correct?

A carbon tax will hurt families who cannot absorb the cost. The tax rebate used by the Canadian Government for residents is in place to offset the increased costs they pay. Where there is no rebate, researchers argue that the wealthy use more carbon-based energy than low-income families do. For example, wealthy people drive their cars while low-income families often rely on public transit. Carbon-tax money that is used to switch public transit to greener energy with electric trains or hybrid buses can keep ticket fares low while gas prices for cars rise.

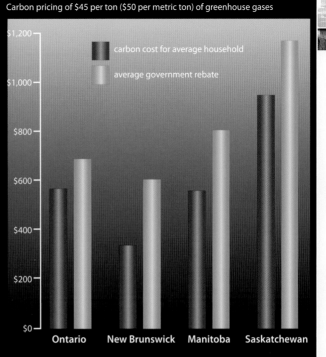

CARBON COSTS VERSUS REBATES
Carbon pricing of $45 per ton ($50 per metric ton) of greenhouse gases

- carbon cost for average household
- average government rebate

Ontario   New Brunswick   Manitoba   Saskatchewan

Typical costs based on proposed carbon pricing system in Canada for 2022

▼ A huge open-pit coal mine. By stopping the use of carbon-dioxide-emitting coal, the environment will benefit. Not only will emissions be lower when coal is burned, but the pollution created as it is mined and transported will also be less.

The idea behind a carbon tax is that it is not the only or final solution. It is meant to encourage the shift away from using fossil fuels. The money collected needs to be used to develop new technologies for more reliable, cheaper forms of renewable energy.

FLOATING ENERGY FARMS

New technologies are being developed around the world. Instead of covering acres of valuable land with solar panels, solar farms are being created to float on oceans. Problems with this new type of solar power generation include allowing the **array** to stay afloat in high waves or storms. Corrosion from the salt water also means different materials need to be used so the panels last.

KEY PLAYERS

Tesla is one of the best-known electric car companies. It not only produces four models of electric cars, but also solar panels and solar tiles. Its mission is to speed up our transition to a sustainable, green ecosystem. Tesla believes that electric cars are just the beginning. Its long-term plan is to create all types of electric vehicles, including trucks and mass transit, as well as batteries and power-generation solutions.

▼ Elon Musk, CEO of Tesla, has created a gigafactory, which will be the largest building in the world when it is complete. It will produce 500,000 electric cars per year. It will be solar powered and an overall zero-energy factory.

WHAT'S AT STAKE?

What steps can individuals take to keep the government focused on developing new technologies to reduce the use of fossil fuels?

▲ Rain forests are natural carbon sinks. They remove carbon dioxide from the atmosphere, so it is vital we keep them. Yet climate change has created forest fires, which then release the carbon dioxide back into the atmosphere.

Carbon capture and storage is another important piece of green technology. Negative emissions technologies (NETs) remove carbon dioxide from the atmosphere and store it. Some NETs are natural, such as planting forests and giant kelp (seaweed) beds in shallow ocean waters, which store lots of carbon dioxide. Human-made systems use filters in chimneys or add **alkaline minerals** to the ocean to pull carbon dioxide from the atmosphere.

STORING ENERGY

Batteries that hold more energy for longer periods of time are a vital part of making wind, tide, and solar energy more reliable. NAWA Technologies is a French company that is developing an Ultra Fast Carbon Battery that it claims stores more energy, lasts longer, and could charge to 80 percent capacity in approximately 5 minutes. Other ideas include silicon, aluminum, and even liquid metal batteries.

It is tempting to become informed about a topic, then think your job is done. But keeping up to date is especially important with topics like carbon tax and climate change. Threats to the environment are increasing rapidly. Our health and even the survival of our planet are at stake. There is a lot you can do to help if you are equipped with knowledge and understanding of the situation.

▼ The High Line in New York City is an old 23-block-long, elevated railway that has been turned into a park. The trees there capture and hold more than 1.3 tons (1.2 metric tons) of carbon each year, reducing pollution in the air.

INTERNET SEARCHES

Make your searches quicker and more accurate with these tips:

- Use quotation marks around phrases to search for that exact combination. Searching for "carbon emission" will give you sites on all news about greenhouse gases and climate change. Searching for "carbon tax" will narrow your search to the basics of taxing carbon.

- Use a colon to limit your search to only specific sites. For government publications on carbon tax, try "carbon tax:gov"

KNOWLEDGE IS POWER

Our understanding of climate change and the role of greenhouse gases are being studied by scientists and researchers all the time. Some benefits or problems related to them come to light only after time has passed. New data allows us to modify the technology needed to address carbon dioxide emissions. Current studies also allow us to compare the effectiveness of carbon tax and cap-and-trade programs. Ineffective results can lead to environmental groups putting pressure on governments to make deeper cuts, raise taxes, or give more support where needed.

SEARCHING OUT FACTS

Finding ways to keep up to date can be a challenge. Not all information is **broadcast** to the public. The results of a new study or the latest statistics do not often make the news. Specifically, the topic of carbon tax is unlikely to catch the attention of mainstream magazine journalists or TV documentary makers. Popular science magazines, such as *Scientific American* and *New Scientist,* and quality newspapers, such as *The New York Times, National Post,* and *The Guardian,* are good sources.

Libraries, government agencies, and industry associations collect information. Environmental groups, scientists, and researchers post their work online. Ideas on limiting our carbon footprint, or stores that sell green energy items, can also be found online. By seeking out new data, you can make sure what we buy and what we do in our lives matches the facts and will have the best, positive effect on the issue.

Today's technology makes it easier than ever to keep up to date. The Internet has sites designed to gather news on a topic. These are called content aggregator sites. Users input keywords on the subject they want to read about. Some aggregators are strictly for news such as News360 or Feedly.

Instead of searching for "carbon tax" news on each search engine one at a time, Dogpile is an example of a site that collects the best search results from multiple search engines. Curator.io is an aggregator site some people use for social media posts.

Some organizations also collect global news on a specific topic. Earthsight reports on environmental crime and injustices around the world. Climate Feedback is a network of scientists separating fact from fiction in the media. You can also set up an alert on search engines such as Google that will send you an email each time your keyword shows up on new articles posted.

CHECK YOUR SOURCES

An important step in gathering current information is to **audit** your **news diet.** Check where you are getting your source material. Be aware of the bias the material might have. Work toward collecting material from a variety of sources for a balanced view. For the issues of carbon taxes and climate change, this will include the fossil fuel industry, environmental groups, technology companies, and the government. Look at the websites of the Carbon Tax Center and Department of Energy (United States), Natural Resources (Canada), and UN-Energy.

Even the most reliable news sources can give false information at times, so it is important to get in the habit of checking the facts you hear. If you find facts that **contradict** one another, dig deeper. Try to find scientific data that backs up one side or the other.

INTERNET SEARCH TIPS

When looking at websites, address extensions can help identify the sources of the information.

.gov (government)—official government organizations or departments. You may not be able to access all areas of these websites.

.org (organization)—usually nonprofit organizations and charities. You may have to register to use these.

.com (commercial)—mostly businesses. This is the most widely used web address extension.

Country extensions:
.ca Canada
.us United States
.au Australia
.uk United Kingdom
.ru Russia
.de Germany

◀ Make a habit of searching for updates in different media—online, in print, podcasts, advertisements, or TV documentaries.

◀ More than ever, we have the ability to get facts and figures from every corner of the world. The skills you learn keeping up to date with the issue of carbon taxes will be useful in getting informed and staying informed about other topics.

GLOSSARY

alkaline minerals Substances from Earth that have a high pH level

array A collection or group of similar items

atmosphere The envelope of gases around Earth and other planets

audit To systematically review or assess something

broadcast Transmit by radio or television

carbon capture and storage The process of capturing carbon dioxide and storing it in a way so that it does not enter the atmosphere

carbon dioxide A colorless, odorless gas that is a component of Earth's atmosphere

carbon footprint The amount of carbon dioxide emitted by one's use of fossil fuels

climate change Long-term shift in Earth's global climate due mainly to human activity

consumers People who buy things

context Setting, circumstances, or background for an event or idea

contradict Give an opposite statement

controversial Causes disagreements

credible Able to be trusted or believed

current Happening now

diesel A type of fossil fuel used in vehicles

economic Relating to the wealth and resources of a country

efficient Working in a well-organized way

emissions Substances discharged into the atmosphere

environment The surroundings in which a person, animal, or plant lives and functions

evidence Information or facts that prove if something is true

exhaust Waste gases and particles expelled from a combustion machine

fossil fuels Natural fuels formed long ago from plant and animal remains

green energy Energy that does little or no harm to the environment

green technologies Technologies that lessen or reverse the effects human activities have had on the environment

greenhouse effect Trapping of heat in the atmosphere, leading to global warming

greenhouse gas Any gas in the atmosphere that traps heat

impartial Treating everyone equally

imported Brought in from another country

incentive Anything that encourages people to buy or do something

Indigenous Describing the earliest inhabitants of an area

infrastructure The basic systems needed to operate something

legislation Laws

media Methods of mass communication such as TV and radio

merit Value or worth

moderate Average amount

motivated Interested in doing something

natural resources Materials that occur naturally in an area and can be used to make or do something

news diet The mix of sources used to get information

objective Not taking one side over another

phase out Stop a process slowly over time

podcasts Audio files available online

policies Ideas, plans, and procedures used to guide decision-making

pollution Harmful or poisonous materials that are introduced into the environment

poverty line The minimum money needed for people to buy essentials

power generation Creating energy to allow machines and industrial processes to work

renewable energy Energy that comes from natural sources that are never used up, such as wind, sunlight, and water

short-term Over a small amount of time

source material Original document or other piece of evidence

statistics Math dealing with the collection, analysis, and presentation of numerical data

summaries Brief statements or lists of the main points

tax rebate A refund to taxpayers after they have paid taxes

turbines Engines that spin to create energy

urgent Needs immediate action

vice tax An additional cost on items considered to be harmful to people or society; Also known as an excise or sin tax

vital Really necessary

SOURCE NOTES

QUOTATIONS

Page 4: https://bit.ly/3n1vkgY
Page 9: https://nyti.ms/3oMaAeP
Page 14: https://bit.ly/3kFBimT
Page 17: https://bit.ly/34Fgje5
Page 25: https://nyti.ms/2TDdR1n
Page 33: https://bit.ly/3kShEDW

REFERENCES USED IN THIS BOOK

**Chapter 1: The Need to Know,
    pages 4–7**
www.carbontax.org/whats-a-carbon-tax
https://bit.ly/2TzlCEH
https://bit.ly/2TzKBsD

**Chapter 2: How to Get Informed,
    pages 8–13**
www.c2es.org/content/carbon-tax-basics
https://bit.ly/31VHrnw
www.nrc.gov/materials/srcmaterial.html
https://bit.ly/3mCffxE

**Chapter 3: Carbon Tax and Climate,
    pages 14–23**
https://tgam.ca/3myMLF7
https://bit.ly/34JjZvH
https://bit.ly/31TG8Fr
https://bit.ly/3kFrXeP
https://nyti.ms/2TAVZEu
www.ipcc.ch
https://bit.ly/37ORBKp

**Chapter 4: Suspending Judgment,
    pages 24–31**
https://taxfoundation.org/carbon-tax
https://bit.ly/31VO8Ga
https://bit.ly/2Jk6YAn
https://bit.ly/3jNK8xH
https://n.pr/3jCn1G1
https://bit.ly/2TC81gU

**Chapter 5: Where Things Stand,
    pages 32–39**
https://bit.ly/2GeszJk
https://bit.ly/2HIAU8y
https://bit.ly/35PjRtC
https://bit.ly/31Tfe0B
https://bit.ly/2J8uyzN
https://bit.ly/37UrCRU
https://bit.ly/2TC8Whe

**Chapter 6: Keeping Up to Date,
    pages 40–43**
https://bit.ly/2TERad6
www.thehighline.org
https://bit.ly/2JkcjHV

FIND OUT MORE

Finding good source material on the Internet can sometimes be a challenge. When analyzing how reliable the information is, consider these points:

- Who is the author of the page? Is it an expert in the field, or a person who experienced the event?

- Is the site well known and up to date? A page that has not been updated for several years probably has out-of-date information.

- Can you verify the facts with another site? Always double-check information.

- Have you checked all possible sites? Don't just look on the first page a search engine provides.

- Remember to try government sites and research papers.

- Have you recorded website addresses and names? Keep this data so you can backtrack later and verify the information you want to use.

WEBSITES

Learn about climate change with NASA:
https://climatekids.nasa.gov/climate-change-meaning
The Center for Climate and Energy Solutions (C2ES) explains climate basics for kids:
www.c2es.org/content/climate-basics-for-kids
Natural Resources Defense Council:
www.nrdc.org/stories/how-you-can-help-fight-climate-change
Price on Carbon.org:
https://priceoncarbon.org/business-society/history-of-federal-legislation-2
U.S. Environmental Protection Agency:
www.epa.gov

BOOKS

Brearley, Laurie. *Water Power: Energy from Rivers, Waves, and Tides*. Children's Press, 2018.

Burns, Kylie. *William Kamkwamba: Powering His Village*. Crabtree Publishing, 2017.

DK. *Dkfindout! Climate Change*. DK Publishing, 2020.

Fleischman, Paul. *Eyes Wide Open: Going Behind the Environmental Headlines*. Candlewick Press, 2014.

McDaniel, Melissa. *Facing a Warming World* (Understanding Climate Change). Children's Press, 2020.

Ziem, Matthew. *Wind Power: Sailboats, Windmills, and Wind Turbines*. Children's Press, 2019.

ABOUT THE AUTHOR

Natalie Hyde has written more than 75 fiction and nonfiction books for kids. She shares her home with a little leopard gecko, and a cat that desperately wants to eat it.

INDEX